Hau
Of Branson

Charles Kennedy RN, PhD

Haunted Hotels of Branson

Copyright 2014 Charles Kennedy RN, PhD

Haunted Hotels of Branson
is dedicated to Robin LaRose
for her hard work editing these stories

Blank

Index

Chapter	Hotel	Page
	Introduction	7
1	The Branson Hotel	9
2	The Gazebo Inn	17
3	Chateau on the Lake	23
4	The Crescent Court	31
5	The Grand Palace Hotel	37
6	Hotel Grand Victorian	43
7	La Quinta Inn	49
8	Motel 6	55
9	Ye Olde English Inn	63
10	Grand Country Inn	73
11	Outback Roadhouse	79
12	Radisson Hotel	85
13	Big Cedar Lodge	91
14	Some Haunted Eateries	99

Blank

Introduction

Haunted Hotels of Branson is a collection of stories about some of the most popular establishments in the Branson area. These stories are based on interviews with guests, employees, and others who have either witnessed the events or have heard from others, what transpired. Unless the story has photographs or other evidence of a definitive haunting based on an investigation by my team, I am retelling, what was told to me.

With all the rich history of Branson I am not surprised by the activity level in the area. Some of the stories suggest that the specific activity is an intelligent haunting. That is to say that it directly interacts with the living although there are some hauntings that appear to be merely residual. A residual haunting is energy imprinted in a set environment that plays over and over much like a VCR in a continuous loop.

Therefore any effort that you make to interact with a residual haunting will not be acknowledged by the spirit.

This tour and book is for anyone who dreams of spending the night or just having dinner with a ghost. Please enjoy the spirits of Branson's most haunted Hotels.

Dr. Chuck

Chapter One
The Branson Hotel

214 W Main Street Branson, MO 65616

Blank

Built by the Branson Town Company in 1903, the Branson Hotel is just a short distance from the Branson train station. It was one of two hotels of the day. The other, the Commercial Street Hotel, was the point of origin of the great Branson fire that destroyed the entire downtown area in 1912. Only four buildings survived the fire, one being the Branson Hotel.

One of the most well known stories about Branson is that of *Shepherd of the Hills*, the tale of how Harold Bell Wright came to the Branson area after being diagnosed with tuberculosis. His intent in coming to Branson was to find a climate that would be better for his health. He stayed with a nice couple, JK and Anna Ross out west of town on highway 76 and initially was only going to spend a day or two with them. As the story goes, he ended up staying with them so long that became the inspiration for the characters, Old Matt and Aunt Mollie in his book, *Shepherd of the Hills*.

Mr. Wright returned to Branson spending many summers with JK and Anna. When he was done gathering data for his book, and needed a quiet place to take out his notebook and create his story, he chose the Branson Hotel. During the day he would sit at his desk in the corner of his room known today as the Notebook Room. In the evening, he would relax on the second floor veranda overlooking downtown as he worked and reworked his tale. He spent quite a bit of time working on his story in that room and soon he began calling the Branson Hotel home. The *Shepherd of the Hills* marks a spectacular turning point in Wright's literary career as the book's success was almost immediate. Millions of copies of the book have been sold in several languages as well its adaptions for four movie versions. Wright's 40-year career as a writer resulted in 19 books, many scripts for stage plays, film adaptions, and a number of magazine articles before his death in 1944. That is one nice writing career he started in that Notebook Room on the second floor of the Branson Hotel.

Recently, I spoke with two guests of the hotel which we will call Tom and Sherry. Tom told me that he and his wife spent three nights in the Notebook Room. The first night was uneventful as far as paranormal activity goes, but on the second night, something woke him up in the very late hours. Awake but having no idea why, he rolled over and tried to get back to sleep. As he began to drift back off to sleep, he heard what he believed was mumbling. Startled because this mumbling sounded like a man, Tom quickly looked over at Sherry who appeared to be sound asleep. But then he heard a sound coming from the corner of the room, the pages from a book being turned.

At that point, Tom was wide awake and his senses completely alert. He threw back the covers, jumped straight up out of bed, and looked frantically toward the sound. There sitting at the desk was a man working on a manuscript but as soon as the man looked up and saw Tom he vanished. Stunned, Tom looked around the room for a few minutes then slowly crawled back into bed wondering perhaps if he had been dreaming.

When morning came, Tom didn't say anything to Sherry not wanting to concern her. He knew they were booked for my Ghosts of Branson ghost tour later that day and decided he would try and get my thoughts on what he had seen. As Tom told me the story, Sherry's jaw dropped as she asked him "why didn't you tell me?" Tom just shrugged sheepishly and that's when Sherry admitted that the same thing had happened to her on their first night in the room. It appears the first night hadn't been so uneventful after all. I quickly dug out a photo of Harold Bell Wright from my files to show them which caused them both to freeze in disbelief. Together they nodded and told me that the man in the photo was indeed the same man they had seen in the Notebook Room during the middle of the night.

From my kitchen window at the Ghosts of Branson office, I can see the balcony on the second floor of the old Branson Hotel. There have been many times late at night when I have seen someone sitting on that balcony reading. I usually run out the back door and race down the alley a block away just to see if anyone is really there. Unfortunately, every time I get to the end of the alley, the veranda is empty. Was it Harold? Was it a guest or staff member? I guess I will just have to be faster one time to find that out.

The Branson Hotel is fully restored and decorated in the period of its prime. If you like the exquisite, early 20th century style of architecture and decor, this is definitely the place for you. And if you don't mind sharing a room with a spirit, then make sure you book the Notebook Room of the Branson Hotel.

Blank

Chapter Two
The Gazebo Inn

2424 W Hwy 76, Branson, MO 65616

Blank

The Gazebo Inn is a lovely turn of the century style inn in the heart of the strip, set back a bit almost to the point of not being noticeable. It sits immediately to the east of Andy Williams Moon River Theater. The many strengths of the Gazebo Inn include clean well kept buildings and friendly courteous staff who strive to make your stay a very positive experience. I have spoken to many guests of the inn who come to Branson often and would never consider staying anywhere else. I believe this to be a glowing tribute to Joel, the manager and his dedicated staff. In fact, often times there may be others at work making sure your stay is much more than the normal hotel stay, because when it comes to spirits, normal is paranormal.

On the second floor of the rear building is a room where one guest checked in and never really checked out. As the story goes two gentlemen checked in one Friday afternoon. They were named Bob and his brother Steve. The plan was to spend a fun filled weekend in

Branson. After getting settled into his room, Bob decided to take a quick nap before hitting the town with his brother. He told his brother Steve to go out to scout out the area that he would be ready to go after a rest. So, Steve left the hotel promising to return with a fun game plan for the weekend. But, later when the Steve returned from his search, he found that his Bob's nap had turned into a permanent condition. The rescue squad was called but it was of no use because upon arrival to the emergency room, Bob was declared D.O.A.

Needless to say Steve left the Gazebo Inn and returned home never getting the chance to spend that fun weekend in Branson with Bob. It was after that weekend I began to hear about guests, especially male guests, who would be startled from sleep in that room when the bed would sink as if someone had just sat down next to them. Some have reported awakening to see a man sitting on the edge of the bed or hear a male voice say "isn't it time to go see the sights?"

Even when a man and woman stay in that room together, it is only the man who the unwanted guest approaches as they sleep. It appears that our now rested spirit is trying to get his brother up to finish their weekend on the town.

The second floor balconies of the Gazebo Inn overlook one of the private court yards of the Moon River Theater. In one of my trips to the building, I was taking pictures of that very court yard. Using a digital camera, I was able to pick up on an IR or a near infrared image.

SIDE NOTE: The Gazebo is right next door to the Moon River Theater set up by Andy Williams, one of the first big name acts in Branson. He first came in the early 90s and helped put Branson on the map as an entertainment capitol. Williams loved Branson right up to his death in September of 2012. When he got sick, he didn't retreat to Los Angeles but rather stayed in his beloved Branson.

Here is the photo that fascinates me the most. If you look at the right hand door over the branches, there appears to be a figure.

Here is a close up of the image. On closer examination, the figure even looks familiar.

All in all, the gazebo is a hot bed of paranormal activity. Enjoy your stay.

Chapter Three
Chateau on the Lake

415 State Hwy 265, Branson, MO, 65616

Blank

Chateau on the Lake is Branson's majestic castle nestled in the cliffs along the eastern shore of Table Rock Lake. It is a perfect venue for the boating enthusiast, as a retreat for corporate meetings and events, and even better for the diehard romantic looking for an elegant dinner with the setting sun over the sparkling waters of the lake. The Chateau on the Lake, prides itself on being the stylish establishment in the area and while much of the Ozarks tries to offer down home country charm, the Chateau radiates class and excellence which entices many a young bride to request it for their wedding reception.

But, there is another facet to the Chateau on the Lake that is quite interesting, it is haunted. So, how does such a high end facility so desired for its charm and location become haunted? Well, that is easy to answer. Spirits show no social partiality. They don't care about gender; race, how much money someone has, and they definitely don't have a problem with age discrimination, so to put it simply, ghosts are *everywhere*. Chateau on the Lake is no exception.

The Chateau was built around 1997 so it is a relatively new venue in Branson which proves spirits non-interest in how old a place is. As the story goes, in the early years of its existence, a young couple planned to hold their wedding reception at the fairytale castle of the Chateau. The ballroom was reserved, gowns purchased, invitations had all been sent out, and the weather forecast was predicted to be perfect. Everything was set and in place for every girl's storybook wedding. Nothing could possibly go wrong.

As the big day approached the bride began to notice that the groom seemed to be distant and somewhat distracted. She writes it off as "groom-to-be jitters" and figures once the ceremony and reception are over, the honeymoon would prove to be exactly as she had always dreamed it would be. But, something happened the night before the wedding during the rehearsal that changed everything.

That night before the wedding, the woman's fiancé came to her with something she would have never expected from her knight in shining armor. The strangely incomprehensible words, "I can't do it" spit from his lips.

In a numbed state, she watched as his mouth moved reiterating his horrible declaration, "I can't go through with it." The once beautiful glow waned from the young woman's face.

"What do you mean, you can't go through with it" she asked as tears streamed from her horrified eyes. If he gave her an answer she wouldn't have heard it because she was sobbing. The devastated young bride collapsed to the floor.

Looking up at her groom, she fought to form the words, "How can this be true? I'm so in love with you." With little hesitation the groom shouted his heartless response for all to hear. "Well, I'm not!" He then stormed off, without any further explanation leaving his shattered bride behind to face the fallout.

There wasn't going to be any dream wedding. What would she tell her family, her friends, and what about the future she had planned around the love of her life? What about her dream of dancing with her dashing husband in the spectacular ballroom of the Chateau on the Lake? Her life was suddenly as cold as the marble floor she was sitting on. As the nausea sets in all she could think about was the pain, the shame, and the disappointment in her parents' eyes. Instead of facing the people waiting for her in the other room, the broken hearted woman ran out of the building and sped off to her apartment.

Later, as the sun set on the waters of Table Rock Lake, the Branson Belle cruised past the Chateau on the bluff where our bride to be, dressed in her flowing white wedding gown lies still. She had swallowed half a bottle of sleeping pills washed down with a Jack and Coke. Drifting off to sleep the vision swirling in her head was most likely the band playing as she and her new husband floated across the ballroom of the Chateau on the Lake. By the time the police found her it was too late. On that beautiful Saturday in May, instead of attending her love filled wedding, her family and friends were faced with planning and attending her sad and dismal funeral.

      Even now there are guests of the Chateau who will question the staff about the wedding in the ballroom. Of course when they are told that there is no wedding on that day, the confused guests insist that they just ran into a bride in a wedding gown on the elevator. They persist that the bride had asked them for the time because she said she didn't want to be late to her own reception.

Blank

Chapter Four
The Crescent Court

311 Branson Landing Blvd, Branson, MO 65616

There is a quaint little collection of cottages, called Crescent Court, that sit just north of the historic downtown district on Veterans Parkway. Many of the cottages rent by the month and are frequented by guests new to the town who are looking for a short term living arrangement until they can set up permanent residence.

Sometime in July of 2007, Terry Lynn Huey, from Harrison, Arkansas, loaned Dewayne Lynn, $30. When Terry went to the Crescent Court cottages to collect the debt, Dewayne told him that he didn't have any money. When Terry Lynn became angry and demands his money, a fight breaks out between the two men just outside cabin 11. The battle quickly escalated and Terry Lynn Huey, 52, pulled out a knife and stabed Dewayne in the chest.

Now, the Crescent Court is just two blocks from the hospital but it might as well had been a million miles away because it was of no help to the wounded Dewayne. Blood streamed down his body as Dewayne stumbled out to seek help. He barely made his way to a bench right outside the office of the cottages when the injury proved too much for Dewayne. Before long he slid off the bench and down to the pavement into an immense pool of his own blood. Before help could arrive, Dewayne died right there on that sidewalk in front of the office.

Meanwhile, Terry Lynn Huey had jumped on his motorcycle and high tailed it down to Arkansas. It was only two days later when he was apprehended and arrested. Lynn was convicted of second degree murder and is presently serving 20 years in prison.

Every now and then when the sound of traffic is distant and the wind is still, guests will hear two men fighting outside the cabins of Crescent Court. But, when they look out the window to see where the yelling is coming from, they see only the shadow of one man, hunched over on the bench outside of the office. As they look more closely, they watch the shadow slowly slide down off the bench onto the pavement then disappear right before their eyes.

Terry Lynn Huey is serving 20 years for second degree murder of Dewayne Lynn over $30.

Blank

Chapter Five
Grand Plaza Hotel

245 N Wildwood Dr, Branson, Mo 65616

Blank

Another hotel in the heart of the strip set back about a block but still visible to the traffic flow, is the nine story hotel, The Grand Plaza. This well kept tower is very popular with Branson's visitors. The general manager, Ray runs a tight ship and is well respected by his team as a true professional. Each staff member feels that an unhappy guest reflects on each of them. For instance, almost all of the hotels in town offer a continental breakfast but the Grand Plaza takes it to a new level.

The view from the ninth floor offers a panoramic look at Branson with the Ozark Mountains to the north and the entertainment strip to the south. At night the lights from the area dancing in the rustling trees is quite a site. The ninth floor Pub on the Plaza is a cozy lounge that is a comfortable place to relax, grab a bite to eat, and meet interesting people.

In October of 2010 a young lady named Stacy thought it would be cool to have her friend meet her at the Pub on the Plaza so she arranged a rendezvous for that Wednesday evening. It wasn't just a friend Stacy was expecting to meet that night but the love of her life. As she sat at the bar her pulse raced in anticipation but quickly turned to horror when she saw who got off the elevator, her heart nearly stopped. Stacy panicked as her ex-husband, Stewart, walked into the Pub. She shot out the side door to the hall and ran for another elevator trying to escape her stalker's eye. But Stacy is not fast enough and Stewart follows close behind. She hurries to her car to drive to a smaller hotel off the strip where she is staying. Stacy darts from her car, room key in her hand and looks back to see if she had been followed. Jumpy, she struggles to put the key in the lock. She was almost safe and in her room but as we all know, when facing death "almost" doesn't count. Stacy felt the stinging blade of a knife sink deep into her back as she reached for the doorknob. Stewart's knife had punctured Stacy's aorta and she was dead before she hit the ground.

So, who was Stacy's mystery man, the love of her life who she was supposed to meet at the Plaza? We don't know. What I do know from talking to several staff members is this. Several nights a week they notice a young lady sitting at the bar or at one of the tables. No one can ever remember seeing her come in but all of a sudden she is at a table and then again at yet another table. Again no one sees her move and then all of sudden, she is just gone. Then suddenly someone sees the woman out by the elevator desperately trying to get on it. Is Stacy still trying years later to meet up with her mystery lover at the romantic Pub on the Plaza? Or is Stacy still trying out run her murderer?

Blank

Chapter Six
Hotel Grand Victorian

2325 W Hwy 76 Branson, Missouri 65616

Blank

The Hotel Grand Victoria is a sharp looking upscale Victorian style hotel right in the heart of the strip. Close to shows, attractions, and shopping, it is an extremely popular base for many visitors. The thing about normal visitors is they usually leave and go home but there is one paranormal visitor that apparently has never checked out of the Hotel Grand Victoria. To make this even more fascinating, this permanent visitor likes to share a room with the current guests. A choice that many of the living guests are not always thrilled about.

Although people generally like their privacy, when it comes to ghosts, privacy is the last thing you can count on. Last year, I ran into Katie and Mike, a nice couple staying at the Victorian. Katie relayed an experience to me of an event that took place just a few nights earlier at the Hotel Grand Victoria about her encounter with a peeping spirit. Here is her story in her own words.

"There was a dresser at the foot of the bed with a biggish mirror. I saw reflected on the mirror a shadow. It was peeking out from the bathroom door that was slightly ajar. The lights were off inside the bathroom but I could still make out a distinct human shape. It was darker than the dark bathroom but it was solid. I stared at the reflection for I don't know how long. I couldn't really tell if it was staring back at me as it had no face (but somehow I had the feeling that it was spying on me). There was just solid blackness where a face should have been. I blinked to make sure I wasn't just seeing things and sure enough, it was still there. I got out of the bed to confront it (honestly, I'm not sure what I was thinking then) but it had vanished. I went back to bed, looked at the mirror again, it was no longer there."

Katie said Mike slept through the whole thing. When she told him of the shadow the next day, Mike just laughed and told her that she must have been dreaming. Needless to say, this just angered her. I then asked if she had felt threatened by the shadow but she replied that no, she hadn't felt threatened. I then asked her if the shadow had tried to harm her or Mike in any way. Again she told me no, it had not. So, I asked what the harm was to which she remarked that she just expected to be alone in the room. I went on to explain that spirits are everywhere so you can never expect to be alone. Mike then told her if she wanted to change hotels they would. I reiterated that spirits are everywhere it's just that certain ones let you know when they are around and that moving to another hotel would not ensure privacy.

Somehow Katie felt better after our talk and admitted she really didn't want to change hotels. She came to the realization that the other hotels probably had their own ghosts and she liked the Grand Victoria.

Katie and Mike finished their stay, then checked out and went home but when she got home, she sent me an email. She thanked me for helping her with her vision and that they had a great time in Branson. She said because of the fun she had at the Hotel Grand Victoria she would always recommend to all of her friends that "when you go to Branson, only stay in a haunted hotel." Well, as you can tell from this book, that is certainly a good possibility.

Chapter Seven
La Quinta Inn

1835 Missouri 76, Branson, MO 65616

Blank

The La Quinta Inn is a nice family friendly motel on the strip but is located right next to the very haunted but friendly City Music Center. It is very possible that some spirits may share the City Music Center and the La Quinta Inn because there is one very popular spirit that is attached to both buildings, the spirit of a little girl. While the employees of the Music City Center have named her Amy, the La Quinta employees just call her "the little girl." Since this book is about haunted hotels in Branson, I will only tell the story of "the little girl" of La Quinta for now.

Housekeepers at La Quinta have reported going into rooms after guests have checked out and as they walk through the door, they hear what sounds like a child humming or singing. When they look toward the sound, they see a young girl by the dressing mirror. Believing a family must be panicked about their missing child, the housekeeper hastens to call the front desk. But when the little girl looks up into the mirror and sees the housekeeper, the little girl looks frightened but then instantly vanishes. The housekeeper stands in disbelief wondering if her eyes were playing tricks on her.

It has happened too often to too many housekeepers so, I have to say no, it wasn't a trick, it isn't stress, and it isn't their imagination. It was the little girl, Amy. We don't know who Amy was and we don't even know why she haunts that location. We only know she visits both the La Quinta and the City Music Center.

Jennifer, a guest who stayed at the La Quinta last year, said she returned to her room after an afternoon of shopping. She opened the door and was surprised to find a little girl facing the dressing area. Amy had spread Jennifer's makeup out across the counter. Jennifer let out a startled gasp causing Amy to spin around. Seeing Jennifer, the little girl vanished into thin air. Jennifer just stood there speechless, unable to move. All afternoon was a daze as Jennifer tried to make sense of what had gone on in that room that afternoon. She knew she had reservations for my tour for that night so she decided to arrive early to talk to me about it.

As soon as Jennifer walked in, she pulled me aside and said, "I have to tell you what happened today." In a nervous excitement, she repeated the story of the little girl in her room. I asked where she was staying and when she stated the La Quinta Inn. I just smiled and told her that she had just met Amy. Her reaction was "you mean I am not crazy?"

I told her "I can't certify that, without further testing but you saw what you saw." After I relayed the stories of little Amy, Jennifer was relieved to find out that others have also encountered this delightful young lady.

Through further investigation we hope to discover who this child was and why she goes from the halls of the Music Center to the rooms of the La Quinta. We may even learn about her fascination with the mirror and the dressing table. Did she get caught playing with her mother's makeup? Did her mother work at one of the locations? We can only surmise for now.

Chapter Eight
Motel 6

Schaefer Dr. south of Hwy 76 Branson MO

Blank

Hidden in Motel Row off the "main drag" is a series of hotels and motels. Among them is Motel 6. As you might wonder, who is really leaving the light on for you? Before the Motel 6 chain bought the hotel, it was the Mountain Music Motel. Back when the hotel was Mountain Music Motel, there was a maintenance man, a gentleman by the name of Lendel. This is the story of Lendel.

Lendel was a big man and was always known for wearing bib overalls, a flannel shirt, a baseball hat, and always had a toothpick hanging from the corner of his mouth. As a loyal employee Lendel was always ready to help. He had a small apartment right in the building and he was available day or night to deal with any emergency. Guests of Mountain Music Motel knew Lendel for his good ol' boy smile and friendly wave. Folks knew they could count on him if there was a problem. But some time around 2005, the good Lord called Lendel home.

His co-workers were stunned. Taken too soon they said. As it turns out one morning there was a leaky faucet in one of the rooms. Lendel's number was called but there was no answer. They tried his cell phone. Still there was no answer. This just wasn't like Lendel. Finally the manager went down to Lendel's apartment to find him in bed. He appeared to have been taken peacefully in his sleep and it was determined that he had probably had a heart attack.

As usual in a high turnover industry, new people came along to the Mountain Music Motel. They all heard the story of Lendel, how everyone missed his help and amusing stories of how he brightened everyone's day. It wasn't long before the new folks felt like they knew Lendel.

Then one day, a man named Tom was hired to take Lendel's place. Tom had some pretty big shoes to fill but he didn't have the experience or the knowledge that Lendel had. But Tom never stopped trying to keep up with Lendels reputation. As calls would come in to the office of reports needing maintenance attention, Tom would eagerly hustle from assignment to assignment. After a while, very odd things began happening which made Tom start wondering about what was going on. It started when Tom would get a work order to go to fix something in one of the rooms. But when he arrived at the room he found that the leaky faucet, the broken lamp, or the loose towel rack had already been fixed. Tom knew he was the only maintenance man, so who was doing the repairs?

Then one day Tom was called to fix a broken bathroom lock. The guests in the room greeted him at the door and said, "Oh the other guy fixed it, it just needed tightening." Tom was flabbergasted. "What other guy?" he inquired. "The big guy in overalls and baseball cap, he spoke softly over his toothpick. Real friendly guy he was" was their reply.

Bewildered, Tom returned to the office to tell his story. He was very distraught as he explained that this wasn't the first time things were fixed before he arrived. When he explained how the guests described who had done the repairs, "Lendel" flew out of the manager's mouth. "They just described Lendel" he said. Tom blurted out "but that's my job now." Everyone but Tom had a good laugh over the fact that Lendel was still around.

  A few weeks later the two front desk clerks were sitting in the office. It was late in the afternoon so very few cars where in the parking lot leaving them a clear view of the whole lot. Joan was preparing papers for guests who were soon to arrive. Christy was just daydreaming as she sat looking out the window. Suddenly she noticed a man standing out in the parking lot waving to her. It struck her as odd because he just seemed to appear as there were no cars around to have let him off. Where did he come from? Christy was frozen in her chair as she looked at the smiling man in bib overalls, a flannel shirt in July, toothpick in the corner of his mouth and a baseball cap. She turned to Joan and questioned what Lendel looked like. Joan put her papers down on the desk in front of her and asked "why?" Christy slowly pointed to the parking lot and asked "is that him?" Joan looked out the window and replied that no one was out in the parking lot.

"No way!" Christy screamed as she jumped from her chair and ran outside with Joan close on her heels.

Christy had never seen a ghost before and started to tremble as she told Joan what she had just seen. Joan tried to reason that because it was at least 25 yards to the nearest building, no one could disappear that fast. They both pivoted in circles looking in every direction. No one was in sight and there were no cars someone could have gotten into.

"Where was he standing" Joan demanded.

Christy says "right about here."

That's when Joan saw it. Lying on the ground, the very spot at where Christy had pointed was a toothpick.

The ladies went back to their desks, speechless. They both knew now that Lendel was still watching over the place and although they had just seen a ghost, they must have felt some comfort in knowing he would always be there for them.

Chapter Nine
Ye Olde English Inn

24 Downing St, Hollister, MO 65672

Blank

The Ye Olde English Inn is one of my favorite places. It is located at number 24 Downing Street in Downtown Hollister, that sleepy little town next to Branson. The English Inn is a mere three minutes from the Branson Landing shopping mall in downtown Branson. The hotel was built in 1909 by William H. Johnson, who at the time was a prominent lawyer from Springfield. Johnson purchased a 100 acre plot along the railroad with hopes of developing a town there. He led the construction with the intent to make Downing Street look like a small English village that he hoped would appeal to the folks getting off the train across the street.

The initial building was a story and a half tall and was made up of the current lobby, stone staircase, the huge stone fireplace, and some guest rooms on the second floor. In 1918 the building was sold to Johnson's son. The next year, the young Johnson started construction on the three story addition which housed the Black Horse Pub and two upper floors of hotel rooms.

In the 1980s, the hotel closed to overnight guests and the second floor sat empty for about 25 years until the building was bought by best selling novelist, Janet Dailey. A great deal of restoration was done to bring it back to its original luster.

Any hotel with this kind of history is bound to have, well, "history" and most assuredly have some paranormal history as well. When the most recent renovation was taking place, Ms. Dailey wanted to make sure the building was secure at night. She hired some off duty police officers to guard the building to keep out the bored and rowdy teens. She had no idea there might be more than teens rummaging through her inn at night. On the first night the guards were to watch the building, Dailey stopped by the inn to speak to the officers. Noting that everything seemed fine, she left her inn in the hands of what she believed to be guards capable of keeping her inn safe from intruders. She made a special trip early the next morning to bring them coffee and thank them for their service. To her surprise, they were nowhere to be found. When she finally tracked them down, she asked them what had happened. They sheepishly beat around the bush but finally told this story.

    At about midnight the officers were making rounds to secure the first floor access points when they heard a noise upstairs. They entered the building quietly and make their way up the staircase. As they reached the second floor the beams of their flashlights danced around the room until both beams illuminated a man hanging from a beam by a rope around his neck. The guards quickly informed Dailey that this was not what shook them as they were seasoned officers acclimated to such crime scenes. They had seen worse or so they thought. They then left to call the incident in and decided to wait downstairs for the patrol car. Where would a dead body go anyway? When the on duty police officers arrived, the guards led the officers up the stairs only to find the upstairs empty. No rope, no body, no hanging, nothing.

Daily's hired guards told her that one of the on duty officers had gotten upset and began making accusations and asked "what are you guys trying to pull here?" But the senior officer who knew the area told them that something seemed familiar about this and after a few moments he remembered why. He told them that back when the hotel was closed, some transient worker, probably homeless and destitute had broken into the inn and that he "hung himself right there" from the same beam the guards had found the body. But then when the guard said to the officer "that's great but where the hell is my body?" the old timer just laughed and said "you never saw a body, you saw a ghost." That was the reason the guards gave Daily as to why they left their post. They told her that they refused to guard a haunted hotel so that they could be made fools. The guards then walked out on Ms. Daily and from that point on she was unable to get any overnight guards to work at her hotel.

Amazingly, this is not the only ghost to be seen hanging out in the English Inn. When I spoke to one of the real old timers, a guy who worked there in the sixties, who had a dad who worked there in the forties, I asked about the little girl that is often heard playing and talking to guests on the third floor. Old Bill chuckled and said, "That particular story goes back to the construction of the addition." According to his grand dad, around the time of the addition, a young girl named Harriet was playing in the water at Turkey Creek right up the road. She slipped on one of the wet rocks and fell, hitting her head.

They don't know if the fall killed her or if she drowned. All they know is she had one nasty head injury.

Apparently all of the stone used in the construction for the original building as well as for the addition, was taken from Turkey Creek where Harriet died. Ever since the opening of the new third floor, in 1919, guests and staff have reported seeing a young girl on the third floor. Some guests report that they are in the hallway and they hear a young girl ask them what time it is. They turn around to find that no one is there. I believe that little Harriet, is Harriet Brazeal, born 1912 and who died in the spring of 1919. Her energy, her soul, her spirit is with the stone she died on and is now is part of the historic Ye Olde English Inn.

My hope is that a new story emerges soon because after speaking to the staff at the hotel, Janet Daily was a much loved, down to earth woman in life. She always remembered people's names and never failed to greet each staff member when she would see them. They all recall fondly how much Ms. Dailey loved the hotel and that she spent a great deal of time there with them. Sadly Janet Dailey passed in December of 2013 after suffering from an aneurism so I will not be able to interview her. Well at least not until I find out where she is haunting.

But, I can't help but hope that someday soon, when the hotel is quiet and the guests are still, someone will catch sight of a lady walking through the lobby and that the lady turns out to be the beloved Janet.

Blank

Chapter Ten
Grand Country Inn

1945 W 76 Country Blvd, Branson, MO 65616

Blank

The Grand Country Inn is one of the most popular attractions in Branson. Not just the inn per se but the whole Grand Country complex. They have indoor miniature golf, specialty shops, a music theater, a great buffet style restaurant, along with a very large indoor water park. Guests can literally stay there and not have to leave the complex at all to have a good time. Well, they would have to leave to go on the Ghost tour. However, some guests don't need to leave just to see a ghost. According to former staff members and a few guests that I have talked to, there are reports of a young boy that haunts the hotel. But first, let me tell you about Melissa.

Melissa was staying there for a weekend of fun. Before going out to meet friends, she went to do her hair in the bathroom with the door partially closed. As she combed through her hair she heard a child humming from the bedroom. Having no children with her, Melissa found this to be very odd. Her first thought was that the walls must be paper thin. But that idea began to waver as the humming got louder and moved about her room. She slowly opened the bathroom door and peaked out. As she stuck her head out, and for a split second she saw a young boy about seven or eight dressed in his swimming trunks standing in the middle of the room. But the door began to creak, and the boy turned to look then disappears. Melissa was stunned to say the least. At first she just thought it was her imagination but as she walked out into the middle of the room, she noticed the floor. There in the middle of the room were the wet footprints of a child. Had he really been there?

Who was this young boy? When I tell this story people usually jump to "oh I bet he drowned in the water park." No, there was no tragedy at the water park as far as I know. But, there was a tragedy of another sort and it turned out that oddly enough, the Grand Country Inn was this little boy's hero. I have a friend in Oklahoma who told me about a boy named Tyler who was seven when diagnosed with inoperable brain cancer.

His parents were devastated and with only a few months to live, Tyler's wish was to go on a family vacation. You see Tyler's parents struggled to make ends meet with all the medical bills and two other children. Upon hearing about Tyler, the church in Tyler's home town held a fund raiser to send the family to Branson. So go to Branson they did. They rode the Duck's, they rode the go karts, they saw Dixie Stampede, but, it was the water park that Tyler loved most of all. Tyler lived a lifetime in those three days in Branson and on Sunday night when they left for Oklahoma it is said that he fell asleep in the car going home wearing his swim trunks.

The next week Tyler was due to start another round of chemotherapy but he asked his parents and his doctor if he could refuse this treatment. He told them that it made him so sick he just didn't want it anymore. The doctor admitted that at best it could extend his life by a few days but it would really take a toll on the quality of those last few days. So, his parents didn't have Tyler go through that final round of chemotherapy. A week later, Tyler slipped into a coma in which he would never wake up. It was only a few days before the brave little boy whose only wish was to go on a vacation passed wearing his Branson swimming trunks. They were after all, his favorite thing to wear.

    You see little Tyler doesn't haunt the Grand Country Inn because he died there. Tyler won't leave because his happiest memories are there. So, as you walk down one of the halls or across your room, if you see little wet footprints or the little boy, say "Hi Tyler, are you having lots of fun?" Because now little Tyler is on vacation forever.

Chapter Eleven
Outback Roadhouse

1910 W 76 Country Blvd, Branson, MO 65616

Blank

The Outback Roadhouse is a popular spot on the strip. Folks often confuse the Outback with the national chain of steak houses. Truth is the Branson Outback has no affiliation with the national chain and never did. It seems that the Branson version started a few years before the chain so they have a right to their name. It is sometimes confusing for visitors though.

The Outback Roadhouse has sort of a unique spirit that haunts the rooms; it's the spirit of a diehard sports fan. I have had a few folks on my tour who swear this is absolutely true. Take Marcia and Jim, to name two, who stayed at the Outback not too long ago. Every time they left the room for meals, shopping, or whatever, they would return to their TV on a sport's channel. Now neither Marcia nor Jim is sports fan so; they just chalked it up to the maid leaving it on. Then one day when they were about to leave they decided to find out once and for all how the TV always ended up on the sport's channel. They hung out for a bit while the maid did her thing.

When she was done they checked the TV and it was on the weather station so they shut it off, hid the remote, and went to dinner. As they walked out the door, they stuck the "Do Not Disturb" sign on the door and off they went. About 2 hours later when they came back, Jim slowly and quietly stuck his key in the door and low and behold as he flung open the door, the room was empty but the TV was on the sport's channel.

The next day Jim called me to book a tour and as we were talking, I heard Marcia in the background telling him to tell me about the TV. So after Jim relayed the story to me, I suggested that when they leave to come for the tour, unplug the TV and let's see what happens. The next evening I met Jim and Marcia on the tour and we talked about the sports fan spirit. Jim told me that before coming to the tour he first put on the movie channel, unplugged the TV, and then hung the "Do Not Disturb" sign on their door. After the tour as they were leaving, I told them to call me after they got to their room and let me know what they found.

About 20 minutes later the phone rang and it was Jim. "Son of a gun" he said, "the TV was on and on a sport's channel. That ghost plugged that thing in."

Since that evening, I have spoken to quite a few people who have run into the same exact thing at the Outback Roadhouse. So, I would suggest that if you're in town and want someone to watch a game with, check out the Outback Roadhouse where its sports, all sports, all of the time. And the best thing is you won't have to share your beer and pizza.

Blank

Chapter Twelve
Radisson Hotel

120 Wildwood Dr S, Branson, MO 65616

Blank

The Radisson Hotel is a large multistory hotel that sits right off the strip in the center of the theater district. Towering in the skyline, it is one of the largest hotels by the strip. It is hard to miss even if you are not looking for it. Over the years, thousands of guests have stayed there, but not all of them have left.

According to some former staff members and guests, the Lady in White is still roaming the halls. Many who have seen her never even sensed that she was just a spirit. They thought that she was just another guest that they passed in the hall. Others thought that she was just a guest riding the elevator with them. As she got onto the elevator she pushed the button for the sixth floor. When the car arrived at six, the door opened and the living turned and stepped aside for the Lady in White to get off but, to their shock they were alone on the elevator. Somewhere between the lobby and six, the Lady in White got off without the elevator stopping, the doors opening, and without anyone seeing.

So, who is this mysterious Lady in White? It's a good question and it is a question that may have many possible answers. I personally have not done an investigation in the building so I am relying on the reports of those who have witnessed the events.

Some say that the Lady in White haunts the 6th floor, in particular Room 612. She may have committed suicide there. It is said that a young woman jumped out of the window in that room to her death. It is reported that she was a very happy, friendly lady, and a regular guest at the Radisson. Individuals that knew her best found it highly unlikely that she had actually jumped and committed suicide. They suspected foul play as she stood to inherit a good sum of money. Today, people report that she wanders the halls in a white gown, searching for those that are responsible for her death. Sometimes, the window in the room is found open in the morning, and dresser drawers are found to be turned upside down but then put back into the dresser. I don't know if the windows actually even open now so if these stories are true, were the windows changed after the event because of the event? There are even reports of eerie, unexplained sounds being heard by guests and staff but I have no evidence to deny or prove these claims. As far as a jumping suicide goes, to date I have found nothing to support this however, tragedies in Branson are often kept low key so it is still very possible.

Another theory circulating is that the Lady in White died in the room from a prescription drug overdose. Again, was it an accident, suicide, or intentional? All we seem to know is that a young woman with so much to live for is gone. Well, almost gone. For whatever reason, her spirit is still searching the halls, rooms and elevator of that stately hotel as she continues to search for answers. Maybe some day if I get to investigate the building, we will find out what her question is and maybe then, we can help her find her answer. Till then, if you are walking through the

Radisson, and you pass the Lady in White, just smile, nod, and as she walks away snap a picture for me. I would love to take this story deeper.

Chapter 13
Big Cedar Lodge

612 Devil's Pool Rd, Ridgedale, MO 65739

Blank

Big Cedar Lodge is one of my favorite all time haunts. First of all, Big Cedar is a beautiful sprawling resort hidden in a private bay on the south end of Table Rock Lake. It is always a pleasure to visit but when you throw in Diva Dorothy it becomes an absolutely amazing place. Let us take a look at the history of this haunt as it explains a great deal about the time, place, and goings on of the area.

Harry Worman and Julian Simmons had no intention of roughing it. The badge of success for the wealthy was called resorting, a luxury escape to the woods without the sweat and bugs. The men developed forest retreats.

Mr. Simmons' house (now Devil's Pool Restaurant) was of a rustic, Adirondack stick-and-log design, with a spiral staircase that wrapped around a standing cedar tree trunk to an upstairs balcony. Furnishings included a black marble onyx bathroom with gold-polished plumbing fixtures.

The men's wives, Madge Simmons and Dorothy Worman, held formal dinner parties for their Kansas City friends who came to spend weekends. Worman's young wife Dorothy, less than half his age, supposedly created quite a bit of talk in the area. One story holds that she showed up at the post office in Ridgedale wearing her swimsuit, which was an unheard of

Dorothy Worman

thing in those days.

A more serious story claims that she had an affair with a member of the staff and ran away with him to Mexico. She soon died there under odd circumstances and was cremated in Mexico, her ashes were sent back to Missouri for burial. Dorothy's pastor held a service at the house and her ashes were scattered at the Devil's Pool grounds.

In 1947, the properties were bought by a California real estate agent who turned the grounds into the Ozarks' first dude ranch, the Devil's Pool Guest Ranch. When Table Rock Lake was finally filled in 1959, covering the famous Devil's Pool spring, fishing boats and outboard motors were provided for guests. The ranch resort enjoyed success through the 1960s, but after changing hands several times the property eventually went idle.

The former ranch was bought in 1988 by Bass Pro Shop's entrepreneur Johnny Morris. He brought his Bass Pro architects to help design the lodge as a fisherman's paradise, to show how a man with vision and money can improve on nature.

The homes built by Worman and Simmons still stand and have been beautifully restored at Big Cedar Resort. Both now function as restaurants. The Worman House Restaurant is a

lovely venue with the main dining room overlooking the bay. It is often the place of choice for parties and reunions. When the group shot time comes for a family photo, the guests are shocked to see that their family photo was photo-bombed by a ghost.

The actual truth about Dorothy's death is difficult to unravel. What is known, however, is that more than a few employees and guests of Big Cedar Resort believe she has returned. There are numerous accounts of a mysterious young woman roaming the grounds late at night. She is usually described as a young woman with brown hair, invariably seen wearing a long white dress. Some say she is sad, others that she is playful and a bit of a prankster. Others claim to have heard her but not seen her. Perhaps the most interesting claims, however, are that she sometimes shows up in photographs taken by guests of the resort, usually as a reflection in the background.

On almost a weekly basis, I get a call from a staff member that has a new story about Diva Dorothy and her need to be the center of attention. Her love of the camera is why I nicknamed her "Diva" Dorothy. Her love of life is evident today as she continues to mingle with the living. As you can see in the photo at the beginning of this chapter, she loves to walk the grounds. I have had staff members tell me that they will have guests come up to them and ask "who is that lady outside in the old clothes?" The staff just cracks a smile and says "That's just Dorothy."

Chapter 14
Some Haunted Eateries

Spirited Dining Experiences

Blank

Mr. Gs Pizza Place

202 N Commercial St, Branson, MO 65616

Mr. Gs Pizza Place is on the corner of Commercial and Atlantic and sits right in the heart of the historic downtown district. For the past 20 years, it has been owned by Michelle.

It's a typical neighborhood pizza parlor/saloon which makes it a favorite for the locals year round. For visitors to Branson looking for the down home feel off the beaten path, this is for you. Be sure to come hungry, because you will definitely love the first rate food offered at Mr. G's. Yes, they have the best pizza but the menu includes something for everyone. You will not walk away hungry. And if you sit at one of the tables by the back wall, you may not be dining or drinking alone.

One night I explained to Michelle that not only was her food superb, her building was fascinating as I was a ghost hunter and found such establishments full of history. She then went on to tell me story after story of strange events that have happened over the years. It wasn't long before we set up an investigation to see what this place had within its walls that might be causing all these stories.

My team arrived about closing time and Michelle and her husband Scott repeated the stories pointing out where the activity had occurred. I started the video cam and Larry Kitzmiller along with fellow team member Robin LaRose proceeded to get baseline EMF readings. The EMF detectors were especially active near the kitchen back by the restrooms.

As the spirit moved around the area he would occasionally sit down but only in the back close to the kitchen. I started recording an EVP session (Electronic Voice Phenomenon). Over the course of an hour or so we learned that his name is Travis and this was once his hangout. I also uncovered that he died of bladder cancer which is usually something I discuss in more detail during my tour.

Before we were through, I had captured several EVPs and two photos of Travis. To hear the whole story, see the photos, plus listen to the EVPs in Travis's own words, take the Ghosts of Branson walking ghost tour and enjoy these spirits and much more. And ladies, Travis will most likely follow you but he is every bit the gentleman.

Blank

The Main Street Deli

111 East Main St Branson, MO 65616

The Main Street Deli at 111 E. Main Street, just up the hill from the Branson Landing, is by far the most active haunted place that I have come across in Branson. The two things that you need to know about the Main Street Deli are:

1. It has the best food in Branson
2. It is very haunted.

In the past year I have done close to a dozen investigations there. It's like going to your favorite fishing spot. You go because you know you are always going to catch something. The first time there we got pictures and EVPs of a seven year old child that blew us away.

But then came time for the research. Why is this place haunted by a seven year old child? Between EVPs and research, I tracked down that little Andrew, was born as Andrew, however his mother was only 18 at the time and unmarried. While just a few days old, his mother gave Andrew up for adoption and his new family changed his name to Carl. Carl lived to the tender age of seven when he joined the spirit world. The reason for his death is hazy, but it may not have been an accident.

In the past 10 months I have gotten numerous EVPs video and photos of little Andrew. Most recently, a Christmas investigation opened up a whole other side to a very sweet little boy who only wants a mommy and daddy.

This story is currently ongoing with more readings and information being gathered as I write. To see the latest evidence and hear Andrew speak, visit the Ghosts of Branson Ghost Tour for a haunting good time. To hold you over till you can make it on the tour, here is a photo of Andrew.

If you have ever questioned the spirit world, this tour will change your mind and heart forever.

About the Author

Dr. Chuck Kennedy has been a ghost Hunter, or Ghostologist as he likes to call it, for over 40 years. His background in neuroscience and the paranormal culminate in a study of the human consciousness both pre and post mortem. In 2012 he put together the amazing walking ghost tour, *Ghosts of Branson* using the Nightshow© Technology, he is able to bring the evidence right to the street so as you walk the dimly tree lined streets of Branson you do not just hear the folklore, but you see and hear the evidence supporting each haunting.

Dr. Chuck can be reached at his web site, www.GhostsofBranson.com

Made in the USA
Charleston, SC
06 April 2014